Joanne E. Bernstein and Paul Cohen

Touchdown Riddles

STURGIS DISTRICT LIBRARY
255 North Street
Sturgis, MI 49091

Pictures by **Slug Signorino**

ALBERT WHITMAN & COMPANY   Niles, Illinois

Also by Joanne E. Bernstein and Paul Cohen

Creepy, Crawly Critter Riddles
Grand-Slam Riddles
Happy Holiday Riddles to You
More Unidentified Flying Riddles
Riddles to Take on Vacation
Unidentified Flying Riddles
What Was the Wicked Witch's Real Name?
and Other Character Riddles

Library of Congress Cataloging-in-Publication Data
Bernstein, Joanne E.
  Touchdown riddles / Joanne E. Bernstein and Paul Cohen ;
illustrated by Slug Signorino.
      p.   cm.
  Summary: A collection of riddles about the game of football,
including "What did they call the naked football team? The
Chicago Bares."
ISBN 0-8075-8036-8
  1. Riddles, Juvenile.   2. Football—Juvenile humor.   3. Wit and
humor, Juvenile.   [1. Football—Wit and humor.   2. Riddles.]
I. Cohen, Paul, 1945–   II. Signorino, Slug, ill.   III. Title.
PN6371.5.B3995   1989   88-21761
818'.5402—dc19   CIP AC

Text © 1989 by Joanne E. Bernstein and Paul Cohen
Illustrations © 1989 by Slug Signorino
Published in 1989 by Albert Whitman & Company,
5747 West Howard St., Niles, Illinois 60648
Published simultaneously in Canada
by General Publishing, Limited, Toronto
All rights reserved. Printed in the U.S.A.
10 9 8 7 6 5 4 3 2 1

To Andy, who loves the Jets. J.B.
To Marie, who hates football. P.C.
To my fine family, friends, football fans, and funsters. S.S.

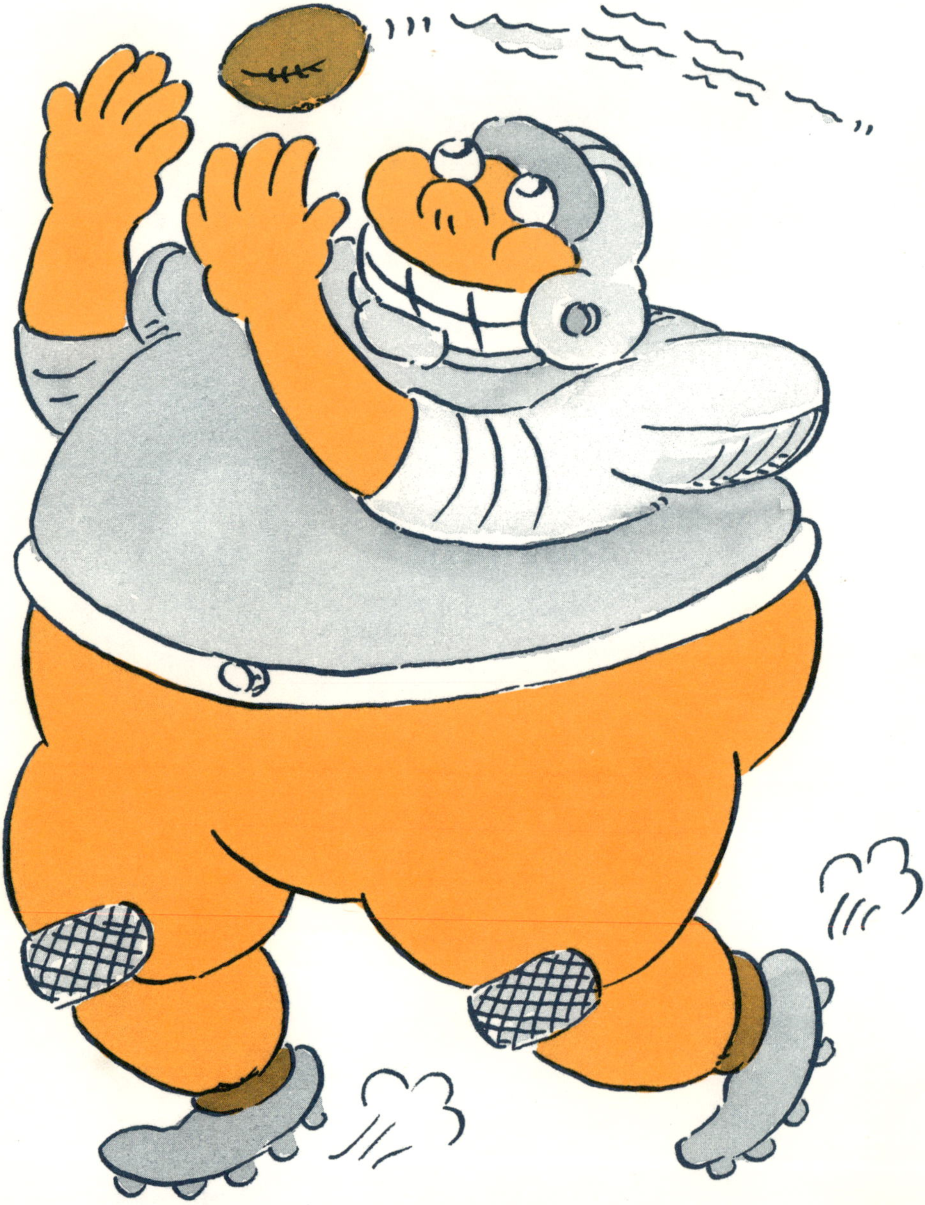

TAKING A POSITION

Who is the fattest player?
The wide receiver.

Who can smell a running play coming?
The nose guard.

Which player never smells bad?
The Right Guard.

Which players have the worst-looking hair?
The split ends.

Which player gives refunds?
The quarterback.

Which refunds twice as much?
The halfback.

Why must the center think fast?
To make snap decisions.

Why do his legs get so tired?
He spends the whole day hiking.

Why does the kicker always carry a spare pencil?
In case he needs an extra point.

And why does the quarterback need a crayon?
For a draw play.

Why did the quarterback have only one hand?
He gave a hand-off to his fullback.

Which player gets the most laughs?
The right tickle.

THE BEST OF THE WEST

What did they call the naked football team?
The Chicago Bares.

Which team has very tiny Vikings?
Mini-sota.

Which LA team can't find its stadium?
The Raiders of the Lost Park.

Why is the soup awful in Kansas City?
Too many Chiefs spoil the broth.

What do you call middle-aged football players?
49-ers.

What team always uses credit cards?
The San Diego Chargers.

Why did they have to go to Buffalo?
To pay all the Bills.

What's often in Denver but always in New York?
The Broncs (Bronx).

THE LEAST OF THE EAST

Where do the Jets go when they feel rusty?
To visit the Oilers.

Which team is most dishonest?
The Pittsburgh Stealers.

What team always wears fresh uniforms?
The *New* Jersey Giants.

Why does Phoenix always win?
It's in the Cards.

How much does corn cost at a Tampa game?
A buck-an-ear.

Where do the Redskins go for advice?
To Kansas City, to see the Chiefs.

Why do Cincinnati players wear orange helmets with black stripes?
To protect their heads.

TIME OUT

How did the musical linebacker relax?
He practiced his sacks.

What would you call an end who runs wide on astroturf?
A carpet sweeper.

What comes after the second period of a Cowboys' game?
The calftime show.

What is pigskin used for?
To hold the pig together.

BOWL ME OVER

Where do football players eat crackers?
At the Souper Bowl.

What's the ants' favorite game?
The Sugar Bowl.

Where do players wear swim trunks?
The Beach Bowl.

Where do great writers play football?
The Prose Bowl.

Where do weevils play?
The Cotton Boll.

What's the bloodiest football game?
The Clottin' Bowl.

Which game puts fans to sleep?
The Siesta Bowl.

GRIDIRON GREATS

Why was the Refrigerator voted heaviest player?
He showed the most yards gained.

What great kicker discovered Florida?
Punts de Leon.

What great quarterback could never figure out which down it was?
Joe No-Math.

What would Bo Jackson be called if he played in LA?
Ram-Bo.

How did John Madden's mother know he'd be a football player?
The hospital gave her a girth certificate.

What did they call it when Pittsburgh's Lynn tripped?
A Swann dive.

What football player is mentioned in the Bible?
O. J. Samson.

Why did Joe Montana bring an antenna to the game?
To improve his aerial attack.

Why was Cinderella such a poor player?
She had a pumpkin for a coach.

What kind of commercial does Alex Karas go round in?
A Karas-sell.

Who's the fastest-talking announcer?
Don Quickie.

Which announcer can you trust the most?
Gifford; he's always frank.

FOOTBALL FAN-ATICS

Why did the Cleveland fan bring a cow to the game?
He wanted milk with his Brownies.

Why did the fans get the Bucs coach fired?
He tried to Tampa with the team.

Who tells the tallest tales about his team?
A Lyin' (Lion) fan.

What do New England fans do on the Fourth of July?
They honor the Patriots.

PLAYING THE FIELD

What play stops a mosquito?
A screen pass.

What offense does the British football team use at 4 P.M.?
The "tea" formation.

Why did the players walk off the field?
The quarterback said, "Hike!"

What kind of notebook does the quarterback use?
A spiral.

MERRILY WE RULE ALONG

How did the referee penalize the goose?
Loss of down.

What penalty was charged to the sick Philly player?
Ill-Eagle procedure.

Why can't barbers play football?
They're always clipping.

Why did the referee take the player's Walkman?
It was an ineligible receiver.

TIME OUT II

What's the best way to stop a Dolphin?
Use the fishing tackle.

Why was the quarterback expelled from college?
He couldn't pass.

Why did the tiny ghost join the team?
He heard they needed a little team spirit.

What did the hungry quarterback do?
He took a roll out.

ZOO LEAGUE

What kind of dogs play football?
The Philadelphia Beagles.

What football team do Philadelphia baseball players like best?
The "Fillies" like the Colts.

Why are the Dolphins so dedicated?
They're a team with a porpoise.

What do you get when you merge Tampa and Denver?
Bucking Broncos.

What play do mice fear the most?
The trap play.

Why can't the Rams play without their cheerleaders?
It's Ewesless.

What would you have if teams from Detroit, Cincinnati, and Chicago came to town on the same day?
Lions and Tigers and Bears, Oh, my!

PLAYERS AT HOME

How do football players get clean?
They have a scrub team.

Who hangs out the towels?
The line.

What do football players call a dozen eggs?
Breakfast.

What do they have with their eggs?
Shredded Cleat.

What kind of homes do "with-it" players have?
They have hip pads.

GREAT FOOTBALL MOMENTS

When Philadelphia won, the headline read, "Eagles Soar." What did it read when they lost?

"Eagles Sore."

What did the papers say when New York was shut out?

"Jets Can't Touch Down."

What headline announced that New Orleans made the playoffs?

"Saints Alive!"

IN THE STANDS

Why is there so much crying in the stands at Cleveland?
It's a multi-tiered stadium.

What would Walt Disney call the Seattle stadium?
The Magic King Dome.

What do they call the upper deck seats in Atlanta?
The Falcony Balcony.

Where do they charge half-price for tickets?
At Fulton Dis-County Stadium.

LIKE IT OR NOT

When is a quarterback like a baseball player?
When he pitches the ball.

Why is a back like a good surgeon?
Both make quick cuts.

Why is a pilot like a quarterback?
They both want to make safe touchdowns.

What's the difference between a camper and a Green Bay runner?
One's a backpacker; the other's a Packer back.

OUR LAST TIME OUT

When do football players sit on their helmets?
When they don't know which end is up.

What comes after the two-minute warning?
A commercial.

Why should you never pay more than $1.00 for a football game?
Because you'll only get four quarters.

Why are referees like the Seven Dwarfs?
They whistle while they work.

Where in the stadium is it toughest to gain a yard?
The parking lot.

What player best closes *Touchdown Riddles*?
The end!

Joanne Bernstein and **Paul Cohen** have been tossing riddles for the Whitman team for the last eight seasons. Joanne's off-the-field activities include teaching education in college and collecting lunchbox thermoses. Paul teaches chemistry and enjoys gardening and travel but can always be found in front of a television set on Sunday afternoons in autumn.

OFFICIAL DISCARD